SIMPLE GUIDES

CUSTOMS & ETIQUETTE OF
ENGLAND

D1115411

ABOUT THE AUTHOR

PETER HOBDAY has had an extensive career in journalism and broadcasting, including 15 years as a presenter of the BBC's flagship daily news and current affairs radio programme 'Today'. He is also author of *In the Valley of the Fireflies* – his own account of life and living in Umbria, Italy, his next favourite place after England. He is today a highly regarded freelance broadcaster and conference speaker.

ILLUSTRATED BY
PETER SEARLE

CUSTOMS & ETIQUETTE OF
ENGLAND

Peter Hobday

Customs & Etiquette of England
by Peter Hobday

First published 1995 by Global Books Ltd.
Second edition 1999
This edition published 2005 by
Simple Guides an imprint of Bravo Ltd.
59 Hutton Grove
London N12 8DS
Tel: +44 (0) 208 446 2440
Fax: +44 (0) 208 446 2441
Enquiries: sales@bravo.clara.net

© 2005 Bravo Ltd.

ISBN 1-85733-387-X

British Library Cataloguing in Publication Data
A CIP catalogue entry for this book
is available from the British Library

Cover image: Image Library Gold Edition
              © Ingram Publishing Ltd.
Set in Futura 11 on 12 pt by Bookman, Hayes
Printed and bound in Hong Kong

Contents

Introduction

'. . . everything ever made . . . recycled at Boot Fairs'

In 1575 the Dutch merchant Emanuel van Meteren arrived in England and it would seem that he was only partially pleased with what he saw . . . On the one hand, he thought the English were a clever, handsome and well-made people, yet he also reckoned they were inconstant, vain-glorious, rash and deceiving. Similarly, he thought we English were hospitable, but like the Germans ate and drank too much. He also decided that we did not work as hard as the French or the Dutch, and, furthermore, were lazy like the Spanish.

He had two other curious observations . . . our servants, he noted, were lazy, and our women well dressed with the habit of sitting outside their doors decked in fine clothes in order to see and be seen by passers-by. Overall, he concluded, like all island races we English were of a weak and tender nature.

The good news is, that in the intervening five hundred years or so, there have been some changes made. Some for the better and some, I am afraid, for the worse. As a native-born Englishman, I hope to set the record straight and not let you fall into the trap of Mr van Meteren and draw the wrong conclusions.

The problem, as I see it, is that the world view of England has been distorted by about 2000 years of fairly successful history: we have won more battles than we have lost; we have made more money than we have squandered; we have tended to keep the good things developed in our culture, and get rid of the bad, and we have managed to compromise with all the great challenges of society.

We have a reasonable justice system, a good, vigorous democracy, and a fair degree of equality, but we have not yet cured the greatest problem of most nations – arrogance: that we believe we are by far the best, that we are blessed indeed to have been born in this nation, and that foreigners can only envy us!

Happily, membership of the European Union has put our institutions under the microscope, and some have been found wanting. One of our great writers and thinkers, Dr Johnson, writing in the eighteenth century, remarked that 'patriotism is the last refuge of the scoundrel'. So I will try to moderate any claims that I make for my country in how it behaves, its customs and manners, and leave it to you, the visitor to our shores (in person or as an armchair traveller), to make up your own mind.

But a word of warning ... almost everything that you come across in England is a result of a long history. Usage, tradition and custom play a central role in almost every facet of public and to some extent private life.

We do not easily discard anything that seems to work, or at least does little harm to anyone.[1] Which is why you will find judges dressed up in eighteenth-century wigs,[2] wearing gowns of red and black, sometimes edged with ermine; which is why if you visit Parliament you will see, in the House of Lords, the Lord Chancellor, the

---

[1] This includes everything ever made, and small enough to put in a car or van, that is recycled at Boot Fairs (usually for relatively little money) held throughout the country in spring and summer. Increasingly, because of the high UK taxes, bootleg spirits and tobacco are also to be found. Similarly, we seem to love driving ancient second-hand cars. In the US, a car boot is known as the trunk; see p. 75.

[2] A 1997 survey revealed that people generally prefer to see judges in wigs: they said they looked more detached and wiser, which is what they should be.

highest law officer in the land, dressed in a frock coat, wearing a full wig and sitting on a huge cushion known as the 'Wool Sack'. The 'sack' is indeed stuffed with lamb's wool to remind the peers that this was once the source of England's wealth and prestige a thousand years ago . . . (But not for much longer, perhaps; the New Labour Government is going to 'reform' the House of Lords.)

Ritual, pomp and ceremony are dear to the English. I firmly believe we arrange better state funerals and coronations than any other nation in the world.

'Ritual pomp and ceremony are dear to the English'

HARMLESS ECCENTRICITY

Of course there are changes. For example, some of our citizens see too much influence on our language and our culture coming from North America. Just look at the way the young speak, dress and amuse themselves, some say; it is all American!

But there are still English travellers who when asked by a desk clerk in a hotel in, say, Washington DC whether they are foreigners, will reply without a moment's hesitation: 'No, I'm English'.

So, welcome visitor; be patient with our little ways, and try to view them as a harmless eccentricity maintained to brighten up the dull and dismal routine that is much of daily life. I hasten to add that none of what I suggest in this book is mandatory, it is only a guide!

Top Tip: Friends For Life

Once you have made a friend in England you have made a friend for life. And that friend will patiently explain all you need to know about the social and other pitfalls in this ancient Kingdom. Friendship is not given lightly, and one should not mistake the natural reserve of the English for coldness. They like to give people time to reveal their true natures and to reveal their own in return.

The English produced William Shakespeare – one of, if not *the*, greatest masters of our language. Shakespeare penned some famous lines about England – lines that used to be learned at some time by most schoolchildren, and they go a long way to explain who we are and what we are. This is what he wrote:

This royal throne of kings, this scepter'd isle,
This earth of majesty, this seat of Mars,
This other Eden, demi-paradise,
This fortress built by Nature for herself
Against infection and the hand of war,
This happy breed of men, this little world,
This precious stone set in a silver sea,
Which serves it in the office of a wall,
Or as a moat defensive to a house,
Against the envy of less happy lands,
This blessed plot, this earth this realm,
  this England . . .

King Richard II, II, i

1

Land & People

'The United Kingdom . . . forged over hundreds of years . . .'

WHAT IS ENGLAND?

Many people are confused about the differ-ence between terms like 'Great Britain', 'United Kingdom' or 'England'. Some believe that they are interchangeable. Historians and others argue otherwise. I must admit that sometimes the inhabitants of these islands off the north coast of continental Europe share that confusion. So let us be clear: this book is about England; it is not about Wales nor Scotland, nor Northern Ireland.

Nor should England be seen as part of the Channel Islands which are closer to France than to England, and which are self-governing, except in defence and foreign policy. Nor do I include those islands off the coast of Scotland – Shetland, Orkneys and the Hebrides. All these bits and pieces are part and parcel of the United Kingdom of Great Britain and Northern Ireland, forged over hundreds of years by war and annexation and presided over by a Royal Family that traces its ancestry in the main back to German and Dutch royalty with various other European nationalities – from Russia, Scandinavia, Austria and Portugal – also making an appearance in the royal family tree.

Top Tip: Remember the 'National' Traditions

Down the centuries, despite the mayhem that produced the ultimate union at the beginning of the eighteenth century (p. 20), the English, the Scots and the Welsh have fiercely kept their own separate traditions and customs, which is why we have our individual national football teams, rugby teams, and athletics teams, despite the fact that a British team could probably take on the best in the rest of the world and give a good account of itself.

As a reminder of the turbulent past, the British army has regiments that retain their Irish, Scottish or Welsh names such as the Black Watch in Scotland and the Welsh Guards.

GAELIC AND CELTIC

The differences between these island peoples is maintained by dialect and accent. Even when the Welsh and the Scots are speaking English they use words which are not found in England, such as 'breeks' for 'trousers' in Scotland. In parts of Scotland there is a different first language which is Gaelic, and some of the music written for that tongue has a lilt and cadence that marks it out as something no English speaker could imitate. Music also separates the Welsh in tone and tradition from England.

The Welsh male voice choir has a sound that comes from the valleys – it is a sound of men (often coal miners working in the most arduous conditions) making music in the face of adversity. The voices are deep and defiant, but melodious and, as in Scotland, resonate with the language. In Wales, too, Welsh is increasingly spoken as a first language and not just in some of the remoter parts; it is also used as a first language in an increasing number of schools. Listen carefully for these national accents; and remember, the Welsh and the Scots very definitely do not like to be called English!

'England, Scotland and Wales'

AFTER THE ROMANS

England is made up of various peoples that were once fiercely independent. About two thousand years ago there were seven principal kingdoms – Northumbria, Mercia, East Anglia, Essex, Kent, Wessex and Sussex. Cornwall was more Celtic than anything else so it formed part of Wales. The Romans tried to subdue the natives, but even a general as capable as Julius Caesar found it a never-ending battle.

In fact, one of his successors, Hadrian, even went so far as to build a wall to keep out the marauding Scots, a fiercesome challenge when many of the clans ('tribes') came together to defend their lands. Over the centuries, through invasion and intermarriage, these different communities and cultures evolved into more or less a single group. After the Romans, the first invaders were the Vikings from Scandinavia. Fighting the Vikings forced former enemies to get together. Later on, even more tribes became allies when the Normans from France (with links in Scandinavia) invaded and defeated Harold at the Battle of Hastings in 1066.

Despite all the warfare and alliances, each part of England largely preserved its own language or dialect, on top of which was now grafted the official court and administration language of Norman French, with Church Latin still the main form of communication between the educated classes. All this fusion of different forms of speech accounts for the richness and flexibility of the English language, a richness and flexibility which helps explain the fact that it is now the main international language of commerce and almost everything else, and has by far the biggest vocabulary of any living language (over 500,000 words).

ENGLISH ACCENTS

The English that is spoken today is largely free of regional dialect, but not accent. The English speak with what is called 'Received Pronunciation' or the 'Queen's English', or 'Educated Southern English' which emerged from imitation of the upper-class tones of 'society' people in London. Because of the English class system, however, regional dialect or accent are often not considered the marks of a successful individual. This is changing because of the national radio and television networks, which call on local people more and more to contribute to their output as the country starts to celebrate diversity. But it is a slow process. Regional accents are also increasingly used in national TV and radio advertisements for what is perceived as added credibility or, in some cases, entertainment value.

The nasal tones of the Yorkshire or Lancashire accent, for example, are still a source of mockery for some southerners, while the country or rural burr (involving what is called the rolled 'r') of the west of England is supposed to mean a lack of intelligence. But such views are fading fast and more and more young people do not attempt to suppress their local accent in the hope of advancing their careers. In fact, increasingly, the old upper-class sound is being overtaken by what is sometimes called 'Estuary English'[3] – a hybrid mixture of the old and the new – a variation, perhaps, of traditional London 'Cockney' (see p. 80). So be warned, some words will be impossible to understand. As in Italy, where local dialect is still widely spoken, most people can translate from the dialect to the Queen's English. So just ask, they will enjoy explaining. (See Useful Words Ch.12.)

---

[3] I.e., relating to those areas of southern England which are close to the Thames Estuary – viz. Greater London, Essex and Kent.

THE ENGLISH COUNTIES & REGIONS

BRITISH OR ENGLISH?

But the confusion over whether we are British or English needs to be explained. The short answer is we are both. As noted earlier, (p.14) up to the end of the seventeenth century the Scots had their own kings busy fighting to stay in power, often involving clashes with the powerful chiefs of the clans . . . sometimes going to great lengths to do so, as we are told in Shakespeare's great play, *Macbeth*. The Scots fought long and hard against English rule, whereas the Welsh tried a more subtle approach to keep their independence. A family of local Welsh chieftains, the Tudors, actually managed to win the English throne for a time, but lost their independence once their rivals (the Stuarts) had deposed them with the arrival of James I (James VI of Scotland) in 1603.

Finally, there was the Act of Union between England and Scotland in 1707 (an early Maastricht Treaty) and the island was now one 'United Kingdom', ruled from London. The island, which is made up of Scotland, Wales and England, is strictly speaking 'Great Britain'. So the rulers started to create the idea of a new nation, that was Protestant, with the Anglican Church as the state religion, and called the individuals Britons to develop a larger loyalty, than to just their own nation.

King Henry VIII (a Tudor)

The term Great Britain also suggests that we were members of a mythical British tribe which was now in the ascendant. During the eighteenth century, when the Industrial Revolution got under way, a form of national brain-washing took place in order to project this new entity on the international stage.

Religion helped to unify the nation because the King by this time was head of the Church of England and the Anglican faith, a status instituted by Henry VIII (a Tudor, 1491-1547) who had declared himself head of the English Church and set the nation apart from the majority in Continental Europe who were Catholic, and saw the Pope in Rome as the principal representative of God on earth. Even today in Northern Ireland (Ulster), the fight against 'popery' is still as real in some quarters as it ever was. In Glasgow, it is religion which defines whether you support Rangers (if you are Protestant) or Celtic (if you are Catholic) football teams.

Top Tip: The Anglican Church

Today, the Anglican Church (Church of England) is less important in the nation's daily life than it was, but it continues to be a force to be reckoned with that can cause a major national debate – for example, when in recent years the admittance of women to the priesthood was first suggested. Women priests are now a fact of life.

ENGLISH CHARACTERISTICS

People often ask 'What is the nature of English-ness? What are the special characteristics of the English people?' In 1998, there was a TV discussion on this subject when a number of 'personalities' were asked to give their views. The famous English cricket umpire, Dickie Bird, now retired, mentioned the following 'key words' which he thought described Englishness: Beer, Honesty, Bulldog-type, Royal Family, Cricket, the Weather, and used phrases such as 'comradeship and friendship', 'not giving up when things get tough'.

On the other hand, a much younger man, the designer Wayne Hemmingway, suggested keywords such as Freedom, Bloody-minded, He-donistic, Tolerance, and phrases such as 'Great diversity between young and old', 'Multi-racial society' and 'Identity crisis'. Jeffrey Richards, Professor of Culture at Lancaster University, offered these key concepts: 'Sense of humour' and 'sense of superiorty towards foreigners – not concealed'. Another contributor mentioned 'stiff upper lip' and the fact that England has no national costume, which is true.

THE NATION'S FUTURE

Union Jack

From the beginning of the eighteenth century, therefore, it was Britain which went on to create an Empire – and lose the American colonies; it was the Union flag that fluttered over forts in India, Africa and many other parts of the world including Hong Kong, (and even today it forms part of the Australian and Canadian flags). Furthermore, it is the Queen who is head of that fellowship of nations that replaced the Empire – the Commonwealth. However, in Australia there are an increasing number of voices urging the country to become a republic and no longer pay allegiance to the British Crown.

In 1998 both Scotland and Wales voted in a referendum to have their own assemblies (parliaments) which will come into effect in 2001; but there are those in Scotland who want nothing less than complete independence. Similarly, in 1998 Northern Ireland voted to have its own assembly as part of its continuing search for a lasting peace among the Catholic community that wants union with the Irish Republic and the Protestant community that wants to remain in the union with Britain.

Each of the nations that forms part of Britain within the union has its own flag ... the red cross of St George on a white background for England, the blue cross of St Andrew for Scotland, and the flag of St David for Wales ... elements of each go into the unmistakable British flag, known as the 'Union Jack' (p. 23).

The flags of England, Scotland and Wales

2

Royalty & Class

England's class structure

To understand England and etiquette you need to understand the class system, from the Royal Family at its apex to the working class at its base. Earlier, I mentioned accent as a guide to class or social background. But there is more to understand. Apart from modes of speech there is also a 'pecking order' that is well known but not always clearly understood.

At the top of this pecking order, of course, is the Royal Family. There are, as I will explain later, many occasions when members of that family meet their 'subjects', as we are called (not 'citizens').

Top Tip: How To Address Royalty

The basic rule when being presented to Royalty is to wait until you are spoken to, and never ask a direct question. Men bow a little, women curtsey – a habit which growing numbers of women find difficult to execute and is beginning to be considered outdated.

At the present time in England there is much comment and debate on whether England, indeed the United Kingdom as a whole, still needs the Royal Family. It is fashionable to be mildly republican. In such conversations, which centre mainly around the failed marriages of Princess Ann and her brothers, the Princes Charles and Andrew, almost any comment is permitted. But it is not thought good manners to criticize the Queen. Although after the tragic and sudden death of Diana, Princess of Wales, at the end of August 1997, many English people severely criticized the Queen in the immediate days after Diana s death for showing lack of compassion and lack of public support for Diana; they thought that the Royal Standard (royal flag) or Union Jack should have been flown at half-mast immediately out of respect (at Buckingham Palace). In general, however, the Queen should always be praised.

A sign of the times is that the playing of the National Anthem ('God Save the Queen') has been abolished in many areas of public life.

Yet it is still customary to stand when it is played. The test of its popularity, and a test it seems to be losing, is when it is played at one of the main sporting events of the calendar – for example, the Football Association (FA) Cup Final at Wembley Stadium in London, or indeed at the various other football cup finals held there. Some supporters insist on singing their own songs to urge their team on, rather than ask God to save the Queen.

Below the Royals come the various classes of society, which despite the modern world and its more democratic and fair-minded value systems, are still as rigidly in force as ever. In terms of social behaviour the further up the social scale you venture, the more rigid the etiquette, the more the social formalities are preserved. The good news is that the foreign visitor is allowed honorary membership of whichever social class he or she is mixing with at any particular moment!

UPPER CLASS

There are three main class divisions in England with some 'in between' variations (such as 'upper middle'): upper, middle and lower or working class.

The upper (also once known as the 'ruling') class tends to consist of people with inherited wealth, and includes some of the oldest families, with many of them being titled aristocratics. This class, through accent and breeding (many marriages are arranged even at the end of the twentieth century), generally manages to keep to itself and minds its own business. Some members are short of cash and have to open their homes ('stately homes' as they are called) to the public, charging an entrance fee. But as Noel Coward put it in a song he wrote in 1938: 'The stately homes of England, How beautiful they stand, To prove the upper classes still have the upper hand.'

Fox hunter and hounds

The Royal family is important, indeed essential, for the upper class, because it defines their position in society. Without royalty there can be no titles, therefore no status, therefore no idea of class or knowing one's place in society. Which is why for them etiquette is of the utmost importance, although they will pretend it is of no consequence. It is a very English affectation to pretend not to care about something one cares about very profoundly. The upper classes are defined by title, but also by their education, and their pastimes which includes the traditional sporting life involving hunting, shooting and fishing, as well as a great deal of horse-riding for both leisure and as a competitive pursuit.

Over 100 years ago, Oscar Wilde once described fox-hunting as 'the unspeakable in pursuit of the uneatable', but still it continues. (Hunt saboteurs have been trying to get the sport stopped; but the battle is not so much to save the fox as a battle between the rich and the alienated and increasingly, the politically motivated.) I should add, by the way, that those who enjoy horse-riding today are by no means confined to the 'privileged' groups: there are now over one million pony owners throughout the country.

Top Tip: Follow The Strict Dress Codes

There are strict dress codes for each occasion, and no matter how much they are mocked, these traditions survive. For example, there is now a very real attempt by some groups to stop fox-hunting, a very upper-class sport, with its red hunting jackets, (but never say 'red', the jacket colour is always referred to as 'pink') and some women still ride side-saddle.

Be sure to check out what you need to wear before a country-house weekend: will you be shooting, or hunting, or fishing, or dressing for dinner on Saturday night, what the staff expect as a gratuity (tip) and so on. It is best to take advice once you know exactly who your hosts are going to be. (See Ch. 7.)

UPPER-CLASS 'RULES'

The upper classes have quite rigid rules about behaviour and social conduct – from where you have your suits made (Savile Row), your shirts (Jermyn Street), your shoes or hats (St James) or your guns (Purdey's). All these shops are in London (or 'in town' as one should say), and all these items represent a kind of class uniform, and each class has similar rules.

It also has to be said that this system is good for business. In the main, tradespeople who benefit from upper-class clients are also usually official suppliers to Her Majesty and are allowed to display the Royal Coat of Arms on their shop fronts. In the case of Harrods in Kensington (the 'Royal' Borough, as it calls itself), they hold the following 'Royal Warrants':

'Suppliers of provisions and household goods to HM The Queen'

'Outfitters of HRH The Duke of Edinburgh'

'Suppliers of china, glass and fancy goods to HM Queen Elizabeth the Queen Mother'

'Outfitters and saddlers to HRH The Prince of Wales'

The Royal Warrant can be applied for if you can provide evidence that the Royal household places a regular order for your product(s). It is, of course, comforting for the nation to know that certain types of jam, shoes, or breakfast cereals, for example, are as popular with the first family as they are with the general public.

CLASS 'SIGNS'

By and large, each member of a particular class can recognize his or her own, by a whole range of signs, dress, accent and political attitude. For the outsider, the social register in English terms is *Burke's Peerage*, where birth and family determine entry. Read the books of Evelyn Waugh for some of the more exotic or particular lifestyles of the English upper classes. Though written in the 1930s, the best is *Brideshead Revisited*, where one of the main protagonists, Sebastian Flyte, would recognize his descendants even today.

Though upper-class life has changed down the years, it is also still remarkably constant in its attitudes and the way it behaves and the way it expects others to behave towards it.

> ## Top Tip: 'Knowing One's Place'
>
> A famous comic sketch in the 1970s is sometimes revived to highlight the fact that there is still an acceptance (some would say it is instinctive) of class divisions in the English psyche. It features three people of different height standing next to each other. The tallest and best-dressed of the three looks down at the smaller man next to him and says: 'I look down on both of them'. The man in the middle, dressed in a suit, turns to the taller man and says: 'I look up to him'. Then turning to the smallest man dressed in working clothes, says: 'But I look down on him'. Finally, the smallest man just says: 'I know my place'.

MIDDLE CLASS

The middle class is broader in its base, encompassing the professional and managerial classes, and the so-called upwardly mobile. It is much less rigid in its behaviour patterns, except for those members of it, who have pretensions to moving further up the social ladder. If such people have the income they may well shop at Fortnum & Mason or Harrods, and buy bespoke (individually tailored) clothes from Savile Row. They may well have been educated at Oxford or Cambridge universities, or at a 'public school' (as the expensive 'private' schools are confusingly called). But even though they are, in the American sense, more laid back, more relaxed, there can be some formality at certain social occasions – for example, a wedding, or a ball for the young daughter who is, as they say, 'coming out', in other words making her debut on the social stage. Some of the very rich middle classes still like to 'launch' their daughters in this way, in the hope that as they make the social rounds they will find a good match for marriage. Once again, the clothes you wear are important; there is less likelihood of a repeat invitation if you wear jeans, T-shirts and sneakers.

WORKING CLASS

Finally, there is the working class (sometimes referred to as the lower class). Here, there are also tribal rituals as in the other two classes. The type of holiday you choose is a good guide: two weeks in either Blackpool in the north-west of England if you are really traditional, or Benidorm in Spain, or one of the Greek islands, such as Kos, for the younger set.

Behaviour, the roles of men and women and so forth, can be as rigid as in the other classes. The notion of 'political correctness' is mocked by both the upper and working classes in England, but vigorously applied by the middle classes and the 'fourth estate' (the press), not least because much of the p.c. world (p.82) is linked to the women's and minorities' movements. There is in some areas of working-class life a snobbism every bit as exclusive as in the highest levels of English society. One small example: never drink wine in a working man's club, always ask for draught (i.e. non-gas) beer.

'CHATTERING' CLASS

There is one other section of society which is called 'the chattering classes'; it is largely made up of those who work in the media – writers, journalists, TV people and academics. The people in this group tend to 'chat' for a living (amongst other things), and take themselves very seriously indeed. They are drawn from all the other classes, but are somewhat apart, and are usually looked down upon by everyone else as of no consequence and the root cause of all that is wrong with the country. They give the best dinner parties, and are useful guests for the evening or the weekend if you want to stir up a little controversy or you worry that your other guests will not have enough to talk about. They have, it is generally believed by everyone else, no manners.

NOUVEAUX RICHES

There is of course another kind of upper class, the very rich, the self-made millionaires – the 'nouveaux riches' – and a curious fact about this class, is that many of them seem to get titles as well. The problem goes back to the reign of Queen Victoria in the nineteenth century when there were fortunes to be made after the Industrial Revolution, when British industry led the world. In recent years, their ranks have been swollen by the National Lottery winners.

The noted writer and lawyer, John Mortimer, creator of *Rumpole of the Bailey* – a wonderfully comic observation of English customs and moral attitudes seen through the eyes of an old-fashioned barrister (lawyer) – once remarked that the basis of all English literature is class – from Chaucer down to the twentieth century. So pick up any piece of fiction by an English author and you will surely gain some insight into English manners.

And where might YOU stand? That question was asked as the title in a book on class published in 1994. It chronicles the British and English obsession with the subject, from a 1949 Gallup survey which found that 43 per cent said they were working class, while 52 per cent said they were middle class. The middle class found this too broad a definition, so they subdivided: 16 per cent said they were lower middle class, 29 per cent reckoned they were middle middle class, while a few, seven per cent, claimed to be members of the upper middle class.

Top Tip: 'Lifestyle' not 'Class'

What is called 'lifestyle' is replacing class to a certain extent, but whether you are a 'yuppie' (young upwardly mobile professional) or a couple of Dinks (Dual Income Couple with No Kids), an English person will also tell you (mostly implicitly) to which class he or she belongs.

3

Honours & Money

An honours award

England is not content just to have a class system, it has also devised an honours system, whereby everyday folk can aspire to the 'purple' (i.e., in simple terms, becoming a 'Lord' or a 'Lady'), whereby people from all classes can be given titles, knighthoods, or awards for services to their profession, their company, society or the country.

There are two honours lists – the New Year Honours and the Queen's Birthday Honours.

The New Year list is largely created by the prime minister of the day, advised by ministers and civil servants. These honours are rewards for services rendered to country or party. Senior civil servants, ambassadors, senior politicians, senior churchmen and women all figure largely in the Rolls of Honour. More recently, the New Labour Government has honoured a much wider group of people, including those in education, sport and the entertainment industry.

The Queen's Birthday list is also drawn up with the help of politicians and civil servants. But Her Majesty does influence the list and can use her own discretion. So do not be surprised if you meet someone with a title in England; 'Sir' or 'Lady' So-and-so will not expect any particular treatment, and if they have any sense of decorum (i.e., sensitivity and good manners) they introduce themselves when necessary without mentioning the honour they have achieved.

There are so many titles conferred today, it is suggested by some that their inherent 'value' has become rather debased. And there are some politicians, especially in the left-wing of the Labour Party, who would like to see the whole system abolished. But that would leave the problem of the old gentry (gentry = traditional 'landed' families) because there are still the aristocratic families, with ancient titles.

THE ENGLISH AND MONEY

Even today many English people believe that there is something faintly disreputable about being in business. Attitudes are changing, slowly, and the young see the need for such change. But, odd though it may seem, this view of business still lurks in the darker recesses of the nation's consciousness. Which is why it is not considered good manners to talk about money, except to complain about the lack of it. You never tell anyone how much you earn, or will earn. In fact, it is good manners to explain how much you have saved buying this marvellous wine, for example, at the local supermarket. The English are deeply suspicious of conspicuous consumption, although this does not necessarily apply to the the increasing numbers of *nouveaux riches* some of whom are very eager to display their wealth.

The answer to the innocent question 'what does your family do?' pinpoints with accuracy your social position. (Sorry, but we are back on the subject of class again!) Success is not the criterion by which one is judged, as in America. So even an upper-class person who is bankrupt , has no home, no prospects, tends to be treated with more respect than the self-made person.

So, be reassured. The class system in England is for domestic consumption only and of no real consequence to the outside world.

Top Tip: Foreigners Are Forgiven Everything

The visitor to England may wonder how on earth to cope with this apparently subtle and complicated matter of social etiquette. I have good news. Foreigners are mostly forgiven everything! Naturally, this generosity of spirit is helped by the self-belief expressed in Shakespeare's *This England* quoted in the Introduction.

4

Politics ...& Sex

The Commons' benches

Broadly speaking, the political system in England (and for that matter in Scotland and Wales) is divided along class grounds, but pretends it is ideologically based. The Conservative and Unionist Party (note the word 'unionist' in the title) has a history of two hundred years or more and sees itself as defending tradition, the landed gentry and the middle classes. The Labour Party, sees itself as the representative of the working classes (whereas the 'New' – Blairite – Labour Party sees itself appealing to 'Middle England'). There is a third group, the Liberal Democratic Party, which occupies the middle ground, an area hotly disputed by the two 'main' parties, as they are called in the media. The partial erosion of class, and the narrowing of differences between all social groups has created a confusing political landscape where each party regularly seems to adopt the policies of its opponents.

During parliamentary debates in the House of Commons (often abbreviated to 'the Commons' or 'the House') certain conventions are observed: one's colleagues are called 'honourable friends' and one's opponents 'honourable lady or gentleman'. There is no applause, a member can only show verbal agreement or dissent, hence shouts of 'Here, here', which signifies agreement.

There is a list of prescribed words in parliament: you cannot call an honourable member a liar, for instance. But that same member might be deemed to be 'economical with the truth'. The Speaker, who tries to control the debate, calls for 'Order! Order!' when members become particularly rowdy, and were the Speaker to get to his/her feet (stand up) then all members must sit down. (The first woman Speaker in Parliament's history, Mrs Betty Boothroyd, was elected in 1992.)

Top Tip: Politics Can Be Discussed!

The televising of Parliament has softened one of the more rigid rules of social etiquette – that politics, as a subject for conversation, is considered taboo. But since like-minded English people tend to socialize, there is little point in discussing politics as all would agree. However, you can discuss politicians and the fact that none is to be trusted. Examples of politicians behaving badly is also acceptable for dinner-table conversation.

Even in its first eighteen months of office, the ruling New Labour Party has produced a number of sex scandals, with MPs (Members of Parliament) resigning for, in one case, a 'serious error of judgement' (alleged homosexual encounter in a public park), or caught in compromising positions – unfaithful to wives, consorting with models or other fantasy figures.

Lady Chatterley and Mellors

Our Continental neighbours, on the other hand, are much more concerned with bribery and corruption, and believe a person's private life, especially their sex lives, ought to be ignored. In fairness to the political classes, the English have always had an odd relationship with sex. As the poet Philip Larkin wrote:

> Sexual intercourse began
> in nineteen sixty-three
> (which was rather late for me)
> between the end of the Chatterley ban
> and the Beatles first LP

Perhaps I should explain the reference to 'Chatterley' because it says everything about politics, class and sex in Britain. The novel by D.H. Lawrence was called *Lady Chatterley's Lover*, in which the lady of the house sought comfort in the arms of the game-keeper, Mellors, because her aristocratic husband was unable to perform his husbandly duties, he having been wounded fighting bravely for his country in the First World War. The language is direct, the descriptions of their love-making frank. The book was banned on the grounds of obscenity, and thus became a classic *cause celèbre* for the English, with the law and politics made a laughing stock for most of the population. The actual court case produced this immortal question from the crown prosecution to a (male) witness called to defend the book's literary merit:

'Is this the sort of book you would let your wife or servants read?'

The case was dismissed, and publication was allowed, but even today in England there are those who no doubt believe that Lawrence, a coalminer's son, was out to destroy all that made England great. The case is now seen as a defining moment in England joining the twentieth century. The date, as the poet Larkin noted, was 1963.

5

Food & Entertaining

Traditional English breakfast

For quite some time, good food and the English were strangers. This may be explained partly by the fact that most young men in the upper classes were sent away to school where they were given a dreadful basic diet, mainly consisting of gruel (a kind of soup), some beer, bread and vegetables. The women, who stayed at home, tended to eat plain food too. The poor, of course, did not have much choice and ate whatever they could find or steal.

There emerged, therefore, certain traditions in English cooking which you can still find today the further you travel from London. For years there usually was not any type of 'starter' (hors d'oeuvre), but increasingly, as a result of the growing 'internationalization' of our diet, partly through greatly increased travel and the impact of the media's exploitation of food topics, 'starters' such as soups and prawn cocktail are now common enough.

Next, comes the 'main' course – meat, usually roasted, less commonly baked in a casserole dish, accompanied by at least two vegetables, usually boiled. There will always be potatoes, and probably carrots and cabbage, or another green vegetable. Over this is poured a sauce, we call gravy, usually made these days from a gravy powder. The last course, usually called pudding or 'sweet', or 'dessert', would involve pastry in the form of a tart, or a pie, filled with fruit. Over this is poured custard, a yellow, sweet sauce, again made from a powder or, increasingly, ready-made from a tin. These days, cheese and fruit are often eaten as an alternative to 'pudding'.

The 'main' course

BREAKFAST

It was the Victorians who developed many of the instant products or sauces. Breakfast more recently was based on the frying pan, with eggs, sausages, bread, bacon, tomatoes, mushrooms, kidneys and a whole list of other edibles, such as 'black pudding'. To this challenging 'mixed grill' you might add a brown sauce. The profusion of sauces, including the famous Worcestershire Sauce, attests to the plainness of the food and the need for something to spice it up. Even today, when there is a much bigger range of food to choose from, the English have kept to one habit, that is sprinkling pepper and salt on every dish. Even in the finest restaurants in the West End of London you can usually tell who are English people, not so much from the way they dress, but by the fact that they sprinkle pepper and salt on the most subtly-flavoured dish!

Note that all these meals are hot dishes, usually very hot in terms of temperature. It is not unusual in some households for meals to be kept warm for hours in an oven. Warmth also extends to the beer which in some old-fashioned public houses or 'pubs' is still served tepid from the barrel. In fact, in recent years, thanks to a successful promotion by CAMRA (Campaign for Real Ale), many more pubs have reintroduced traditional 'from the wood' or 'barrel' (draught or non-gas) beers. Cold beer is beginning to make an appearance, and ice, too, is used in liquer drinks. But do not count on it. (See Ch. 6.)

Top Tip: Mmm ... Marmalade!

Nowadays, the traditional English breakfast and the heavy midday meal have given way on both health grounds and convenience to less substantial meals. Breakfast is more likely to include a choice of breakfast cereals, fruit juices, toast, tea or coffee. Marmalade (which is available in a huge variety of preparations, from a very sweet jelly-type form to a thick, dark mixture incorporating chunks of cooked orange peel) is put on the toast, all other jams or spreads banished by tradition from the breakfast table!

EATING OUT

Is it any wonder that a country so unused to the finer cuisines of the world, should welcome with such enthusiasm the fast foods (we call 'take-away') of the United States – the burger, the pizza and the chicken bits all now reign supreme. But it is not all bad news. The nation's once rigid and unyielding culinary practices have been relaxed more than somewhat partly because the English are more widely travelled and so tastes have changed.

There has also been a huge influx of foreign styles – Chinese, Greek, Turkish, Thai and Indian – and these are among the cheapest and most frequented eating places in England today – in some cases pushing the local fish-and-chip shop out of business. And this has had a marked effect on the country's reading habits, with cookery books often topping the best-sellers list for weeks at a time. It has also produced a variety of TV cookery programmes which have made stars of their host chefs. The English have now successfully turned the subject of food into a very profitable form of 'entertainment'.

But most of the best food, it has to be said, will be found in the main urban centres, London for sure, then Manchester, Birmingham, Liverpool, or Leeds and York. Though here again, the further you travel from London the more likely you are to find a traditional fish-and-chip shop (although it is true to say that, in general, you will find at least one fish-and-chip shop in every town in England). The English prided themselves on the plainness of their food and in the eighteenth century mocked foreigners – particularly the French – for their liking of snails and frogs' legs. But even these have found their way into the English way of food.

Top Tip: Patience Needed When Eating Out

Today the visitor will frequently find a truly universal menu to choose from when eating out. But when lunching or dining with an English person you may need patience. Half the time they do not quite know what the name of the dish implies, not least if it is in French. But good manners demands that you do not try to explain (except very subtly), since this would imply a criticism on their level of sophistication, and perhaps cause embarrassment.

KNIFE AND FORK

There is a French saying which could be translated as 'while the English have good table manners, the French know how to eat'. And it is true that while the English diner attempts to push peas onto the fork, the French diner will turn the fork upwards and use it more as a spoon, thus enjoying the food while not bothering too much with the etiquette involved.

Using a knife and fork

Too many English people, for comfort, still try to eat everything with a knife and fork, (the fork held with the prongs facing down in the left hand, and the knife in the right) and dislike the American and Continental habit of first cutting food held in place with the fork in the left hand while the knife in the right hand does the business. Then the knife is put down, and the fork moves to the right hand to carry the food from the plate to the mouth. More and more young people, however, have adopted this sensible habit, but in some of the more conservative corners of England such habits are considered common (meaning 'undignified' or 'working class'), or foreign, or both.

But if you lunch or dine in some of the London Clubs (still mostly a male preserve, although a few have moved into the twentieth century and now admit women, the Reform is but one example of this new trend) you tend to see members eating in the time-honoured fashion. And eating the traditional dishes of meat and two vegetables.

The younger generation are much more relaxed and no longer dress for dinner. But again, in some parts of England a dinner jacket is *de rigeur* (essential), and it is as well to check the dress code before you go. Usually, when an invitation is sent, the dress code required will be made clear. A printed invitation invariably means a formal evening. 'Black tie' is the phrase. Do not expect to eat well. The food tends to be monotonous and in tiny portions. Other invitations for a less formal occasion will specify 'Lounge Suit'.

Top Tip: Food on Your Plate – The Unwritten Rule

The English never cease to wonder at the amounts of food served in America; equally, American visitors are often astonished at the small amounts of food served in England. In England there is an unwritten rule that you clear your plate, and that it is wasteful in the extreme to leave anything uneaten. So a small portion works to your advantage if you have a small appetite.

DINNER INVITATIONS

Invitations to a meal in someone's house usually means a relaxed evening. More often than not men do not wear business suits, while the women wear comfortable rather than fashionable evening clothes. It is a good idea to take some flowers or a box of chocolates for your hostess; some, additionally, bring a bottle of wine. It does not have to be an expensive wine, it is, as we say, the thought that counts. The bottle is hardly ever opened, and quite often serves as a bottle that tonight's host takes as a guest to next week's dinner somewhere else.

In most parts of England (certainly amongst the middle and upper-middle classes) the hostess expects a short letter of thanks for the evening. Such letters follow a standard formula: you mention the food (how good it was) and the company (how interesting it was) and express the hope that you will meet again soon. The latest fashion is more for a picture postcard (usually from some cultural spot like the National Gallery) with the same kind of note on the back. Traditionalists still expect and write a letter.

TIPPING & 'SERVICE'

In restaurants the main problem is tipping; some waiters have been known to virtually demand a tip – up to about 15 per cent. But recently there has been a swing against such generosity. Some restaurants even put the service on the bill without asking whether you have had the service you want or wish to reward. Some customers are refusing to pay, and consequently the restaurants have stopped adding this 'service tax' to the bill.

Top Tip: The English and Service

'Service', this is a concept that the English do not always understand. So, if you find yourself waiting rather a long time for your meal, or your bill, or you were not satisfied with the meal for whatever reason, a little bit of complaining goes a long way. The English, renowned for their 'stiff upper lip', sit it out. The foreign visitor is indulged. But it generally pays to complain.

In fact, one curiosity about the English is that the service sector tends to provide very little service. Whether it is a hangover from the days of Empire is an open question, but the native-born English person does not take very kindly to providing a service, even though up to the Second World War, considerable numbers were 'in service' in the Great Houses, with, as the celebrated (1970s) TV series *Upstairs, Downstairs* showed, as strict a pecking order downstairs as anything above stairs. In many service establishments, the employees still have to learn that there is a link between the success of the establishment, and hence their job, and the way they make people welcome and try to help them.

In the 1990s there has been a resurgence of interest in housekeeping and butlering as a job option, with a growing market prepared to pay for such services, especially the new 'executive families' where both partners are pursuing a professional career.

Hotel commissionaire . . . 'providing a service'

6

The Pub

'Was it a pint, or a half, sir?'

For many English people the pub, or public house, is still the centre of their social lives. Pubs have some wonderful names. You can drink in 'The Queen's Arms', 'The Woolpack' or 'The Eight Bells' or pop round to the 'Green Man' for a 'quick one'. A 'quick one' usually means a 'half' or half a pint. Some say a 'swift half', meaning a pint! There is a pub called the 'Lamb and Flag', another the 'Winston Churchill'.

Throughout the country you will find dozens of pubs with the same name. The variations, however, are endless, and typically you will find a painted sign swinging above the door. 'The Tabard' in Southwark, for example, was mentioned by Chaucer in his *Canterbury Tales* six hundred years ago. There is a pub in Bury St Edmunds, in Suffolk, which boasts it has the smallest bar in the country – only three people at a time can get in to be served!

On the other hand, the 1990s have witnessed a considerable rebranding of pubs in an attempt to interest a younger clientele. Bizarre names such as 'The Slug and Lettuce' replaced old favourites such as 'The Pig and Whistle' and 'The Royal Oak'.

But the word 'pub' now includes a huge range of environments in which to drink, eat and relax. Let us start with the most traditional. The country 'pub' is the heart of village life. Some of them have been there for hundreds of years, and some have thatched rooves, and wisteria growing round the door. There is a real coal or log fire in winter, and you can sit out in the garden in the summer. They are welcoming places, with the 'regulars' usually only too happy to talk to the visitor. For most people this is what the pub should always be like.

In the city centres, however, pubs can be much more anonymous, huge drinking places where no one knows anyone, and does not want to know them.

Top Tip: The Secret of Drinking Good Beer

Buy a copy of the *Good Pub Guide* if you want to visit the most interesting places in the country, and you will know not only what each pub is like but what beer they serve, whether it is 'from the wood', that is traditionally brewed draught beer, or whether it is from the 'cask', – a gas or pressurized beer, more the product of technology rather than nature.

Ice and refrigeration have made their appearance in England, but the beer, and other drinks, can still be luke-warm even on the coldest days in some places. Most pubs offer a complete range of beers, local and imported, with German, Belgian and French beers being in demand. The traditional English pint, either 'mild' or 'bitter' is still widely available, but it is giving way to lager, a much lighter 'Continental' beer. Indeed, so popular has lager become, that those who over-indulge, and go on the rampage are called 'lager-louts', now a fairly general insult to anyone who cannot hold their drink.

'PUBLIC BAR'

Many pubs have various sections: the more traditional the pub the more likely you are to find the 'Public Bar'; this is the least comfortable, and in theory should be cheaper. Then there is the 'Snug', usually a small comfortable bar, with a blazing fire in winter. The 'Saloon Bar', was seen as the upper-class section of a pub. Nowadays, many of the dividing walls have been knocked down, and there is just one huge bar and drinking area, plus, perhaps, a dining area.

Various games, especially darts, are also a common feature of pubs; many of the old country pubs continue to promote traditional games, such as 'Bat-and-Trap' (found in Kent) which have been played for hundreds of years (but vary according to region).

Pubs are not only for drinking. Under the influence of the 'Continent', (which, as you will have noticed, is the word we use to refer to the rest of Western Europe, on the other side of the

Top Tip: The Pub Bar

Traditionally, the English stand at the bar to drink, only women, it seems, sit on the bar stools or use the traditional tables and chairs. This used to be a rigid rule, but as mixed drinking has become much more acceptable and fashionable, everybody uses the bar stools and tables.

English Channel) there is now a huge range of bar snacks, and lunches – usually fried fish, or scampi, or sausage and chips, or steak, or the so-called 'ploughman's lunch' which is a great wedge of Cheddar cheese, some bread, some pickle, and an onion. Wine-drinking has also grown considerably in recent years; and 'wine bars' are found everywhere.

LICENSING LAWS

The minimum age for drinking alcohol is 18. Young children, however, cannot go into a pub (although they can go into the pub's garden if there is one), but over the age of 14 they can when accompanied by an adult. What is more, since the reform of the licensing laws,[4] which govern opening times, they are free to remain open all day, so that there is actually no need to touch any alcohol at all – you can drink tea or coffee instead.

---

[4] The licensing laws used to be very rigid, restricting 'opening hours' from 11.00 am until 2.30 pm and in the evening from 5.30 pm to around 11.00 pm. (There were even fewer 'opening hours' on Sundays.) This meant that everyone who bought a round of drinks, just before closing time, had to drink up in the ten minutes of drinking time left after 'time' (often accompanied by the sound of a bell) was called. Although pubs are now able to open all day (but not after 11.00pm unless the publican obtains a special 'extension' of the licensing hours from the local licensing officer for a particular reason, such as a World Cup win, or a Millennium celebration), some still observe the quaint old ways of rationing drinking time, so customers continue to drink against the clock, especially in the evening.

7

What to Wear

Country clothes and a university don in ceremonial clothes

The English love uniforms, and I am not thinking particularly of the military variety. Just look at the great occasions of state, such as the State Opening of Parliament, when the Queen travels in the state coach, dressed in her royal robes, and makes a speech from the throne in the House of

Lords, to the assembled ranks of their Lordships (and Ladyships) who are dressed in ermine cloaks, bishops in red, the military with all their medals, the judges in full wig and gown, and the Members of Parliament from the 'other place' (as the House of Commons is called in the House of Lords), in morning suits. But it does not have to be a state occasion. Just as colourful, for example, is the procession of the Judiciary to the Law Courts, like the Old Bailey in London, at the start of a new law term. University Dons (lecturers) love wearing their ceremonial gowns, at degree ceremonies, and it seems the older the university, the more colourful the gown. In the older regiments of the Army there are any number of dress uniforms for any number of occasions (see front cover).

But even in normal life there is a tradition of uniform, of conforming to certain dress codes. From wearing one's old school tie, to the colour of one's shirt, a person's background can be registered. As Shakespeare put it in *Hamlet*, 'the apparel oft proclaims the man'.

Women are fortunate in being able to look good whatever they wear and are indulged in a genial, gentle, chauvinist way for any eccentricity of dress. Not the men. Even though the world is changing, and fashions are looser and brighter, ultimately the Englishman watching the national summer sport of cricket at Lord's, the home of the game, will wear the exclusive (hardly flattering) club tie, of the MCC (the Marylebone Cricket Club whose home ground is known as

'Lords') and a regulation straw panama hat and even a blue blazer on the hottest of days. It is also *de rigeur* to wear jackets and ties at Henley for the Royal Regatta, if you are a member of the exclusive Leander Rowing Club, and even in the Royal Box at Wimbledon's Centre Court, especially when Royals are in attendance, it is jacket and tie.

The difficulty is knowing when to be formally informal or just modern. The key is whether a member of the Royal Family is attending. Then the more formal and traditional you are the better. Nobody has ever tried to go to a Royal Garden Party in anything other than a dark business suit or a morning dress (even though it is afternoon). And all the women wear hats.

Regulation panama hat at Lord's. . .

But if you want to get your name into the papers and perpetuate the myth that foreigners do not have the same breeding as the English try wearing jeans. They will no doubt let you in if you have the proper invitation – it would be bad manners to refuse you – but I doubt that anyone would wish to be seen talking to you in case bystanders thought you were friends.

There are certain dates in the calendar where everyone knows what to wear. At the annual Lord Mayor of London's Banquet in November when he takes office, for example, it is white ties for the men and tiaras for the ladies. First nights at the opera are also black-tie affairs. (Formal dress would not be required, of course, in the less expensive seats, where lounge suits would be acceptable.)

But, as already noted, the key is often whether the Royals will attend however fleeting their visit may be. Sometimes the Royal only stays for a few minutes; even so, you must dress for the occasion just as you would were they to spend the whole evening or day with you. Happily, the English, in their wisdom, have worked out a code of knowing when a Royal will be on hand or not. This is called 'The Season' and it deserves a section of its own.

8

The Season

Sailing at Cowes and the Badminton horse trials

There is a great deal of debate about what now constitutes the so-called 'English Season'. The marketing departments of so many companies have got involved with their hospitality tents and invitations to such an extent that old-timers shake their heads and mutter that they simply do not know what is happening to the England they knew and loved.

Most of the Season is based on a sporting event, though there is just enough culture to make it seem a wholly more serious period of the year than you might suppose. Among the sporting events that 'one' cannot possibly miss is the Oxford and Cambridge Boat Race along the Thames from Putney to Mortlake (March), the Horse Trials at Badminton (May), Derby Day (June), and Racing at Royal Ascot (July), Tennis at Wimbledon (June/July), Rowing at Henley (July) and Sailing at Cowes (August).

Then there is the Chelsea Flower Show (May), and for the culture vultures, the Royal Academy Summer Exhibition, Opera at Glyndebourne (May–September) and the last night of the Proms (Royal Albert Hall) where you can wave the Union Jack and sing *Land of Hope and Glory* and *Rule Britannia* in an explosion of good-natured patriotism (September).

At other times there are ceremonial events like The Trooping of the Colour in June. (The English Tourist Board has all the details.) For some people, the aim is to go to as many of these events as possible in an orgy of fun and frolic. It is very expensive to do many of these things, and the hiring or buying of the appropriate wardrobe will cost you hundreds of pounds.

The majority of people, however, look upon all of this with mild amusement and do not take it too seriously. But, by and large, there is a 'uniform' that is worn at each occasion, so if you want to be 'in' rather than 'out', it is best to check before you go. In general, you drink plenty of champagne, and eat lots of salmon mousse, and cucumber sandwiches. (At Wimbledon, it is strawberries and cream.)

Dressing up for Ascot

Many of these events are now exploited to the full by business interests, whose main purpose is to wine and dine actual or potential clients with a view to getting more business. This is called 'corporate hospitality'. Purists argue that this has undermined the very nature of what was the upper classes and the rich at play.

Top Tip: If You Go To Ascot. . .

If you go to Royal Ascot, be prepared: men wear top hats and full 'morning dress', while women must wear hats (sometimes the designs are very flamboyant) and dress as daringly as they can to attract attention. The Queen is invariably in attendance, but beware, if you choose to back her horses their win record is not particularly good!

9

Personal Relationships

'. . . always try to praise the animal of the house . . .'

In French and other languages there are what is called the respectful or the intimate use of a verb. The second person plural is the form that denotes respect, the second person singular denotes family or other close relationships. These are the 'Tu' and 'Vous' forms; you can also find them in Italian, Spanish, German and the Scandinavian languages. Rich though the English language is, 'You' can be either plural or singular, and means little else than what it stands for.

FIRST NAMES & FRIENDSHIP

It used to be the case that everyone stayed on very formal terms using Mister (Mr), Mrs or Miss (now mostly superseded by the innocuous p.c. term 'Ms') and it was only when one moved to first-name terms that a certain intimacy was established. Now, following the growing world-wide practice inspired largely by the American cultural tradition, most people move to first-name terms almost immediately without even establishing whether they like each other, let alone want to spend more time with each other than is strictly necessary. Consequently, there are times when the foreigner in England presumes too much from a relationship and is surprised when the English person seems to pull back and withhold his or her friendship.

At worst, this reserve is seen as cold; at best, it is put down to bad manners. Despite the many changes taking place in English life, the new fashions, the adoption of a more open and relaxed way of doing things, Americans particularly are often nonplussed when, after a great evening in someone's company, their 'new friends' never call again.

A more usual occurrence is when visitors to England telephone from the airport to say they have just arrived and can they come over as was suggested 'when we all met up in the States (USA) last month'; they hear mumbled excuses about being 'awfully busy' or not 'convenient' at the moment. Some professions are more welcoming than others. Journalists, actors, and politicians tend to keep open house, accountants, lawyers and doctors tend to keep relationships on a more professional level.

I do not know whether it helps, but even the English are sometimes confused these days about relationships. The best advice is not to push, take your time and you will usually find that once you have made a friend you have made a friend for life.

Even in such elegant shopping streets in London like Oxford Street, 'barrow boys' (even if they are girls) still have their 'pitch' where they are licensed to sell a range of items from fresh vegetables to tourist trinkets. (Some are not licensed and therefore fined for illegal trading.)

Top Tip: Don't Be Offended, 'Love'!

If there is still some formality left in professional relationships, there is one area which often surprises foreign visitors and that is the familiarity that tradespeople use, especially traders in the street markets that are still held in various towns and cities, the most famous of which is probably Petticoat Lane in London. Do not be surprised to be called one of the following names: 'Love', 'Duck', 'Dear', 'Lovey', 'Chuck' or even on occasions 'Sweetheart' or 'Darling'. It is a tradition lost in the mists of time, and no one, regardless of age or gender, should take offence.

PETS

For many English people, animals seem to be more important than human beings in terms of the affection that is lavished. Indeed, some believe that there is more support for the Royal Society for the Prevention of Cruelty to Animals (RSPCA) among the public at large, than there is for the Society for the Prevention of Cruelty to Children (SPCC). The animals' society gets Royal approval, the children's society did not bother with the backing of the Crown.

There are many stories of cats and dogs being left large sums of money by doting owners. There are cemeteries galore for household pets, and the sale of pet food is enormous. There are also very active groups who will even try to harm people they see as experimenting on animals in order to bring publicity to their cause.

In addition, the late 1990s have witnessed increasing public opposition to animal abuse in the food industry – whether it be chickens or veal calves. Members of the so-called 'animal rights' movement have been increasingly aggressive in promoting their agenda. Using live animals for research in the cosmetic industry is now banned.

Top Tip: 'Love Me, Love My Dog'

In terms of etiquette, always try to praise the animal in the house, even if it keeps jumping on your lap and trying to lick you!

CHILDREN

It is a disquieting fact that far too many English people still believe the old maxim that 'children should be seen and not heard'. The boarding school was an English invention designed to relieve hard-pressed parents from having to look after their children or having them around so much that their own lives were disturbed or interrupted. But it is a fact that many English people seem embarrassed by their children in public. In many a restaurant you will see parents trying to get a bored young child, (even a baby) to keep silent and *not make a fuss*. On the other hand, due to an increasingly 'open' approach to parenting, there are also children who tend to be more spontaneous and communicative with visitors to the home – assuming they can be persuaded to switch off their TV or computer and agree to say hello!

Avoiding a fuss!

Only very few parents want or are able to send their children to private schools (about 7%) in order to have freedom to pursue their own interests. . . or because they choose what they believe to be a better education for their children. The system has created one of the country's most successful exports – the English nanny, trained to replace mother and father, and in some circles loved much more.

10

Doing Business

Stock Exchange and Bank of England

So much of English business is owned by American capital – the Americans are the largest single group of foreign investors – that the main way of doing business is very much along American lines. Some even joke, half seriously, that England is the 51st State, because we (the British) have invested more in the States than anyone else, our cultures run on similar lines, that in many ways the two nations are closer than any other two peoples. Maybe.

Remember, however, that the second largest foreign investors are the Japanese, so an important section of industry has a rather more Japanese approach. And, as always, just to confuse the situation, now that we are a part of the European Union, our biggest market is across the Channel, so Continental habits are catching on as well.

Top Tip: The Right Approach to Introductions

When you first meet, there is the usual round of handshakes just as the French do, a light shake, not the hearty version beloved of the sporting types. At first you listen and try not to interrupt, displaying almost old-fashioned good manners with 'thank you' and 'may I please'. As the relationship progresses then it becomes more relaxed and less formal. But, as already noted, do not rush to first names, a little patience in this department will pay dividends.

Nevertheless, the vast majority of businesses are small enterprises and it is here that you will meet the most English of habits in doing business.[5] Above all you will need patience. It is sometimes said that while Americans are sold

---

[5] SHOPPING HOURS
Most high street shops in England open at 9.00 am and close at 5.30 pm. Small town and village shops usually close for lunch between 1.00–2.00 pm; the bigger stores in the main towns and cities remain open all day. In London, and other big cities, there is a Late Night Shopping day every Thursday with most stores staying open until 7.30/8.00 pm. Sunday trading is now available between 10.00 am and 4.00 pm but is largely confined to DIY stores, garden centres and supermarkets.

something, the English buy. So do not expect to be *sold* anything. It is all very understated and you can wait a long time if you think they are going to try and explain the value of their product or service. You actually need to ask.

Beware when doing business with some of the more traditional firms. It never ceases to amaze some visitors to London that tailors in Savile Row still can take two months or more to make a suit and wait even longer before the customer pays.

Of course, a lot of business is now functioning fully in the twentieth century and more than ready for the twenty-first. Management has become tougher and less 'class'-based. The lawyers have made great inroads into the business world, as have accountants. And financial rules and regulations, plus surveillance in the money and stock markets has been considerably tightened up. The City of London's 'Square Mile' is one of the world's three most important trading and financial centres.

Top Tip: Punctuality Counts

Keeping appointments on time is essential (whether business or leisure); it is definitely not considered polite to arrive early (other than a few minutes) or late. Punctuality, like Big Ben, chime together in all English contexts.

Business lunching and dining, by the way, is still a feature of English commercial life. In London, business lunches tend to be lighter whereas in the City, lunches tend to be shorter, more a sandwich at the desk or a working lunch. As for the business dinner, at long last, wives or partners are being invited, which has at least improved the conversation if not the food.

One last point, most of England's trade union leaders have changed a great deal: gone is the old class battle, a tougher breed of no-nonsense, well-educated but dedicated leaders are in place. Get them on your side and business will flourish, as the Japanese have found.

11

The Language

'. . . keeping a straight bat'

English is the most widely spoken language in the world. But there are many forms of English, such as American English, and Australian English. And you can find words in New Zealand and Canada, too, which are home grown and would not be understood in the so-called 'mother country' or by other speakers of the mother tongue. There used to be a lot of snobbery in England about these 'foreign' forms, and many a writer delighted in condemning what they saw as the corruption of the mother tongue by mere colonials.

'ESTUARY ENGLISH'

Happily, that state of affairs is behind us, hopefully for good. Indeed the young in England today show a marked willingness to use the language in a way that inevitably shocks the older generations, but which enriches the language enormously. At the present time there is a great debate over a particular style of English used by young people. Labelled 'Estuary English', it is a mild London (part 'Cockney') and Essex accent with some notable sounds, like the non-pronunciation of the final 't' and 'g' in words, and of the glottal stop, where the 't' in the middle of a word is not pronounced.

'Estuary' is classless (although some would argue that it is very working class), which is what upsets professors and other educators who say it is not 'proper' English. This new, classless accent now includes many American imports. Whereas once it was chic to use a French word, now it is cool to use an American word. Although we in England have absorbed many of these new expressions, and found them very useful indeed, we have allowed ourselves to keep a few of our own which even the most fluent speakers of English might wonder at (see pp 74-76).

'CRICKETING ENGLISH'

Top Tip: Understanding 'Cricket' English

One key to understanding 'English English' (sometimes called 'British English') is to understand the national summer game of cricket. Understand that and you will understand words or phrases such as 'keeping a straight bat', or when something is 'not cricket'. These expressions, like those in baseball in America, are used as examples of what is acceptable or not acceptable forms of behaviour.

You 'keep a straight bat' which means you play the game of life fairly and properly. When something is 'not cricket', it means that the rules are being broken, traditions flouted, in fact someone is probably cheating.

On the other hand, to be on a 'sticky wicket' needs a bit more explaining. Part of the charm of the national game is that the weather is one of the players – the heat or the damp, the wind or the rain over a five-day game can change the fortunes of a side quite dramatically. Suddenly, the ball in the air moves in a different way, spins off the ground in a dangerous fashion, especially when rain has made the playing area, the 'wicket', damp or even muddy – or 'sticky'. So, to find yourself on a 'sticky wicket' means you are in a difficult situation.

'COCKNEY ENGLISH'

Another area which can confuse is Cockney rhyming slang. As the name suggests, you use a word which rhymes with the word you should ideally use. Apples and pears rhymes with 'stairs'. Let's have a 'butcher's', is let's see. Butcher's is short for 'butcher's hook', and rhymes with look. Other well-known examples of rhyming slang are: 'trouble and strife' (wife) 'dog and bone' (phone). It has to be said that a lot of rhyming slang is made up on the spur of the moment and is not traditional.

There are still a few dialect words. In the Midlands, for example, 'bosting' (pronounced 'boss-ting') means 'very good'. And some Midlanders still talk about a child holding its mother's 'donny' or hand. In the North East they talk of 'bairns' meaning young children or babies. And if you ask a Yorkshireman how he is, he might reply 'no but middling'.

There is still some discussion about the concept of what the writer Nancy Mitford called 'U' and 'Non-U' language, meaning upper class and non-upper class. For example you do not say 'toilet' you say 'lavatory' (or possibly 'loo'). You do not say 'serviette' you say 'napkin'. You can still come across these affectations, but as I mentioned earlier, some of it is to do with social class to which the speaker believes he or she belongs. It really does not matter to most people.

Top Tip: How To Say 'Sorry'

One of the most useful words in the English language is 'sorry'. You will hear this used all the time. For some reason, best known to themselves, the English, as a nation, seem to apologize a great deal as much for imagined discourtesies as for real injury. Sometimes the apology can mean 'I did not hear what you said, would you repeat it'. Sometimes it is used to start a sentence such as 'Sorry, but I really must go.' To which is added: 'Sorry to have stayed so long.'

I recall a newspaper cartoon of Concorde flying low over a row of houses whose rooves have just been blown off by the supersonic 'bang'. The pilot, with a huge moustache, is leaning out of the window saying to the houseowners below, all sitting up startled in their beds: 'Sorry'.[6]

---

[6] It is interesting to note that one of Elton John's early hits was called 'Sorry Can Be The Hardest Word'.

'POLITICALLY CORRECT' ENGLISH

English is catching up with the notion of political correctness so new, non-gender-specific forms like 'chair' instead of 'chairman' or 'chairwoman' are preferred. 'Person' is another word that is widely used, instead of man or woman. The etiquette for formal written forms of address now requires the use of Mr, Mrs or Ms. The older terms Miss (for an unmarried woman) and Esq for men have largely disappeared. 'Girl' is a word to be avoided unless referring to a very young female. 'Woman' is more acceptable than 'lady', but some women prefer 'lady'; on the other hand, most men are entirely relaxed about being addressed in the traditional way as 'gentlemen'. So the jury, as the Americans would say, is still out. The general rule would seem to be, when in doubt, leave the gender out.

For the moment, there are not too many traps in the language when race or ethnicity are the subject-matter. Common sense should prevail. We all know when we are being offensive. Some words are still acceptable in England, which are less acceptable in the United States. For example, we still refer to 'Black' people in England, and the word does not give offence. Though many in the Black community prefer 'Afro-Caribbean'. There are race laws in Britain and any language that incites racial tension is a punishable offence. It can be a difficult area. Recently, there was a court case in England which found that Irish jokes can give offence to the Irish community.

12

Useful Words

Despite the influence of American English there are still some words which the people of this island use which can confuse the foreign visitor. I offer the following selection:

Police. The forces of law and order go under a variety of names, from the widely used 'copper' or 'the old bill', to the less used 'bobby' or terms of abuse such as 'the fuzz'. Crime also breeds a vocabulary of its own, so if you are in prison you are doing 'porridge' or 'time' or 'bird' or you are 'inside'. The warders are commonly known as 'screws'.

MEAL TIMES & TERMS

On a happier note, there is some confusion among the English about what to call the various courses at mealtimes. Some insist on French words: 'hors d'ouvres' for example; but in some places the first course continues to be referred to as 'starters' (p.46). The same goes for 'dessert', which is French while most English people prefer 'pudding' or even 'afters' or 'sweet'.

Top Tip: Getting The Meal Names Right

There is some confusion about the terms for the meals. Dinner in some parts of the country, especially in the north, means the midday meal. (Schools throughout the country use the term 'dinner' to describe the midday meal.) On the other hand, in the south if you are middle class, 'supper' is the usual term for the evening meal, unless it is a bigger and more formal occasion, in which case it is called 'dinner'.

The working class everywhere tend to call their evening meal 'tea', usually eaten early evening, and not to be confused with the traditional kind of tea. The mid-morning coffee or tea break is often referred to as 'elevenses' because of the time of day that it is taken.

The English passion for drinking tea continues to play a central role in our way of life; whereas 'afternoon tea', with cakes and thinly cut cucumber sandwiches, is now largely a memory of more leisured days enjoyed by the Victorian middle classes. However, it continues to be available in hotels and 'tea shops' throughout the country, as do 'cream teas', i.e., lightly-baked scones (cut in half) covered with a good topping of thick cream and strawberry jam.

For the sporting fraternity most words are fairly obvious in their meaning. But remember, it is always a 'game' of football, while in cricket it is a 'match'. Cricket matches can last for up to five days, so there are 'end-of-play scores', meaning where the game now stands. The 'result' in a cricket match is when the match is over.

In politics, the traditional Labour Party is on the left, and uses words like 'Comrade', or 'Brother', or 'Sister'; these words are also used by trade union leaders when referring to colleagues, or subordinates. However, the so-called New Labour Party under Prime Minister Tony Blair is much closer to the centre, and as a result some people have referred to it as the 'New Conservative' party, especially as it has adopted many of the Conservative policies, including privatization. Mr Blair likes to be called 'Tony' and the structured informality of the government is part of his 'New Britain', 'Cool Britannia' agenda.

Many phrases, such as 'economical with the truth' (p.44), have come out of 'Whitehall', the word which is used to refer to the whole government machinery of England. The senior civil servants are always referred to as 'mandarins' because of their inscrutable facial expressions. The 'mandarin' characteristics were really brought home to people in a celebrated TV series called

Yes, Minister, in which whenever the civil servant said, with a smile, 'Yes, minister', viewers knew that the minister was about to be thwarted yet again by what is called 'the old boy network' which really runs the country. All visiting politicians to England, as well as their staffs should get hold of a video of *Yes, Minister* if they really want to understand the workings of Whitehall.

The popular press has a vocabulary all of its own. *The Sun* newspaper has coined many new words, or at least the meaning of those words. For example, 'Romp' now almost always means sexual intercourse. An unmarried couple nearly always live, not in a house or flat (the English word for 'apartment') but a 'love nest'.

'Scrooge' or 'Miser' tends to be applied to the Chancellor of the Exchequer (the finance minister) when on Budget Day he raises taxes on what all headline writers call 'booze, fags and motorists'. The word 'fag' is still widely used in Britain to mean cigarette, even though its other more abusive meaning referring to homosexuals can be heard as well.

Some phrases have lapsed, such as 'Old boy', and 'top hole', for example. Others are used very sparingly: 'First class' used to be a compliment, but in these increasingly egalitarian times, it is mostly avoided — to be replaced with 'well done', or 'very well done', or even 'excellent'. Even a simple word like 'yes' seems to have disappeared, to be replaced by 'very much so' or 'certainly'.

TRANSATLANTIC VOCABULARY

What follows is a list of useful words which will help American visitors and American speakers to cope with the 'unorthodox English' language (or 'English English' as it sometimes called) which the English still insist on using:

ENGLISH	AMERICAN
baby's dummy	pacifier
back garden	yard
bill (in a restaurant)	check
biscuit	cookie
block of flats	apartment building
bonnet (of a car)	hood
boot (of a car)	trunk
braces	suspenders
bum	butt/fanny
bumper	fender
candy floss	cotton candy
chemist	drug store
chips	fries
cinema	movie theater
courgette	zucchini
crisps	chips
cross roads	intersection
cupboard	closet
curtains	drapes
dinner jacket	tuxedo
estate agent	realtor
estate car	station wagon
film	movie
flat	apartment
flyover	overpass

give a lift	give a ride
glow-worm	lightning bug
high street	main street
jug	pitcher
jumper	sweater
knickers	panties
lift	elevator
lorry	truck
off-licence	liquor store
oil	lube
pavement	sidewalk
pedestrian crossing	crosswalk
petrol	gas/gasoline
phone me	call me
pictures	movies
platform	track
post	mail
queue	line
to queue	to stand in line
railway	railroad
rubber	eraser
rubbish	trash
shopping centre	mall
sweets/chocolates	candies
take-away	to go
tap	faucet
taxi	cab
tele	TV
torch	flashlight
track-suit	sweatsuit
traffic light	stop light
trainers	sneakers
tramp	bum
trousers	pants
underground/tube	subway

vest	undershirt
video recorder	VCR
wireless	radio
weekend joint	cut of beef for Sunday

Spelling can also be different; for example, English words ending in 're' become 'er' in American; thus the English 'centre' becomes 'center' in American. Similarly, 'our' words become 'or' in American, such as 'harbour' (English) and 'harbor' (American). English 'through' can be written as 'thru' in American.

Facts About England

England is part of the United Kingdom of Great Britain and Northern Ireland (see Ch. 1) which is a member state of the European Union. England covers 130,423 sq km and has a population of around 49,000,000.

The capital of England is London with a population of around 7,000,000. Other major cities include the country's most important port, Liverpool (500,000), and the industrial centres of Birmingham (920,000), Leeds (450,000), Manchester (448,000) and Sheffield (545,000).

There are no wide fluctuations of temperature in England, which on the whole has a moderate climate, although the north is slightly cooler than the south of the country. The west coast has more rain than the east coast. The table below gives the average high and low temperatures (degrees C) and the average number of rainy days (in bold) for London, which is in the South East of England.

Jan	Feb	Mar	Apr	May	Jun
06/02 **15**	07/02 **13**	10/03 **11**	13/06 **12**	17/08 **12**	20/12 **11**
Jul	Aug	Sep	Oct	Nov	Dec
22/14 **12**	21/13 **11**	19/11 **13**	14/08 **13**	10/05 **15**	07/04 **15**

Although England cannot be described as mountainous, very little of the country is entirely flat. Scafell Pike, in the Lake District (in the county of Cumbria), is the highest peak in England at 978m (3208 ft). Other hill ranges of note are The Mendips and The Cotswolds in the west, and The Pennines which run like a spine dividing the North of England.

About 75% of England's land is farmed, although the undulating landscape does not permit as much intensive agriculture seen in other European countries. Sheep and dairy farming predominate in the hilly areas of the North, while the flatter areas of the East and South, sheltered from the worst of the rain from the Atlantic, are ideal for arable crops, such as cereals and vegetables.

Religious Celebrations and National Holidays

New Year's Day	1 January
Good Friday*	March/April
Easter Monday*	March/April
May Day – first Monday in May	May
Spring Bank Holuiday – last Monday in May	May
August Bank Holiday – last Monday in August	August
Christmas Day	25 December
Boxing Day	26 December

* Variable according to the Church Calendar

England has a widespread, privately-funded railway system which generally operates efficiently although can sometimes be prone to disruption by the weather in winter. The Eurostar high speed train connects London to Paris, France, and Brussels, Belgium, using the tunnel beneath the English Channel, in a time of approximately three hours and two hours forty minutes respectively.

Road traffic in England (and indeed the rest of the United Kingdom) travels on the left unlike the rest of Europe. There is a widespread network of motorways, nearly all free of charges, although certain river crossings (bridges or tunnels) within these motorways have tolls.

London has its world famous Underground system which provides quick and efficient travel throughout the city. There is generally a good bus or tram system in all major cities and most towns throughout the country.

The English currency is the pound which is equal to 100 pence (or pennies). The denominations are £50, £20, £10, and £5 notes and £1, 50p, 20p, 10p, 5p, 2p, and 1p coins. Credit Cards are widely accepted in England and

Travellers' Cheques are easily cashed. Restaurant prices do not include service unless stated and tipping is customary. However, beware the practice of automatically adding service to your bill or Credit Card voucher.

Bank opening hours in most towns are 9.30am-4.30pm Monday to Friday and 9.30am-1.00pm on Saturday. Most High Street shops are open between the hours of 9.00am-5.30pm Monday to Saturday although in provincial towns they might well be closed for an hour at lunchtime.

Post Offices usually open between 9am and 5.30pm Monday to Friday, and between 9am and 1.00pm on Saturdays, although there may be a variation on these hours dependent on the size of the town. The post boxes in England are red and are widely distributed.

The Anglican Church is the official state religion, but there are representatives of almost every world religion in England. The Protestant tradition accounts for 55% of the population and Roman Catholicism 10%; Muslims account for 2% while there are sizeable numbers of Jews, Hindus and Sikhs. (For more details of these religions please see the companion series *The Simple Guides to World Religions*.)

Education is compulsory in England between the ages of five and 16.

THE TELEPHONE SERVICE

Public telephones are widespread and take coins and telephone cards, which may be purchased from Post Offices and some shops, such as newsagents. Some phones in large towns accept Credit Cards. There are today a number of telephone companies.

The emergency telephone number for Police, Fire and Medical Assistance is 999.

Index